Title: Jobs in High Demand for 2025: Navigating the Future Workforce Landscape

Disclaimer

Copyright © by Francis K. Pitts 2022. All rights reserved.

Before this document is duplicated or reproduced in any manner, the publisher's consent must be gained. Therefore, the contents within can neither be stored electronically, transferred, nor kept in a database. Neither in Part nor full can the document be copied, scanned, faxed, or retained without approval from the publisher or creator.

Table of contents

Disclaimer
Synopsis
Introduction:
1. Artificial Intelligence (AI) and Machine Learning Specialists
2. Safeguarding the Digital Frontier: The Vital Role of Cybersecurity Experts in 2025
3. Data Analysts and Data Scientists:
4. Healthcare Professionals:
5. Renewable Energy Specialists:
6. E-commerce and Digital Marketing Professionals:
7. Remote Work Facilitators:
8. Blockchain Developers and Cryptocurrency Experts:
09: Environmental Scientists and Climate Change Analysts:
Summary

Synopsis

As we step into the technological and economic evolution of the 2020s, the job market continues to undergo profound transformations. Industries are shifting, technologies are advancing, and new skillsets are becoming paramount. The year 2025 is poised to witness a significant demand for specific roles that encapsulate these changes and cater to the emerging needs of various sectors. Let's delve into the jobs that are expected to be in high demand by 2025.

Introduction:

The job market of 2025 is poised to undergo a profound transformation, shaped by technological advancements, evolving industry landscapes, and shifting societal priorities. In this dynamic environment, specialized skills will be in high demand, reflecting the growing influence of digitalization, sustainability, and innovation across various sectors.

This article explores key trends and professions that are expected to experience significant demand in 2025. From cybersecurity and data analysis to renewable energy, remote work facilitation, blockchain technology, environmental science, and data privacy, professionals with expertise in these areas will play pivotal roles in driving forward-looking initiatives and addressing global challenges.

Moreover, the importance of adaptability, continuous learning, and a proactive approach to embracing new technologies cannot be overstated. As industries converge and new opportunities emerge, professionals must stay agile, update their skill sets, and collaborate effectively to thrive in this dynamic job market.

Let's delve deeper into the specialized skills and professions that will shape the job market landscape of 2025.

1. Artificial Intelligence (AI) and Machine Learning Specialists

With the integration of AI and machine learning into diverse fields like healthcare, finance, transportation, and customer service, the demand for specialists who can develop, implement, and optimize these technologies will soar. AI engineers, data scientists, and machine learning architects will be instrumental in driving innovation and efficiency.

The Rise of AI and Machine Learning Specialists: Pioneering Innovation in 2025

In the ever-evolving landscape of technology, Artificial Intelligence (AI) and Machine Learning have emerged as transformative forces across industries. As we look ahead to 2025, the demand for AI and Machine Learning Specialists is set to skyrocket, driving innovation, efficiency, and competitiveness in various sectors.

The Role of AI and Machine Learning Specialists
AI and Machine Learning Specialists are at the forefront of developing, implementing, and optimizing intelligent systems that can learn from data, make predictions, and automate tasks. Their expertise is instrumental in harnessing the power of data to derive actionable insights, enhance decision-making processes, and drive business outcomes.

Key Responsibilities

1. **Algorithm Development:** Specialists in AI and Machine Learning are adept at designing and refining algorithms that power intelligent systems. They develop algorithms for tasks such as pattern recognition, natural language processing, image recognition, and predictive analytics.

2. **Data Analysis and Model Building**: These professionals analyze large datasets, extract meaningful patterns, and build predictive models using machine learning techniques. They employ tools like Python, R, TensorFlow, and PyTorch to create models that can make accurate predictions and recommendations.

3. **Deployment and Optimization:** AI and Machine Learning Specialists are responsible for deploying models into production environments and optimizing their performance. They fine-tune algorithms, conduct A/B testing, and implement feedback loops to continuously improve model accuracy and efficiency.

4. **Ethical and Responsible AI:** With the growing importance of ethical AI practices, specialists in this field ensure that AI systems are developed and deployed responsibly, considering factors such as bias mitigation, fairness, transparency, and accountability.

As we step into the technological and economic evolution of the 2020s, the job market continues to undergo profound transformations. Industries are shifting, technologies are advancing, and new skillsets are becoming paramount. The year 2025 is poised to witness a significant demand for specific roles that encapsulate these changes and cater to the emerging needs of various sectors. Let's delve into the jobs that are expected to be in high demand by 2025.

Introduction:

The job market of 2025 is poised to undergo a profound transformation, shaped by technological advancements, evolving industry landscapes, and shifting societal priorities. In this dynamic environment, specialized skills will be in high demand, reflecting the growing influence of digitalization, sustainability, and innovation across various sectors.

This article explores key trends and professions that are expected to experience significant demand in 2025. From cybersecurity and data analysis to renewable energy, remote work facilitation, blockchain technology, environmental science, and data privacy, professionals with expertise in these areas will play pivotal roles in driving forward-looking initiatives and addressing global challenges.

Moreover, the importance of adaptability, continuous learning, and a proactive approach to embracing new technologies cannot be overstated. As industries converge and new opportunities emerge, professionals must stay agile, update their skill sets, and collaborate effectively to thrive in this dynamic job market.

Let's delve deeper into the specialized skills and professions that will shape the job market landscape of 2025.

1. Artificial Intelligence (AI) and Machine Learning Specialists

With the integration of AI and machine learning into diverse fields like healthcare, finance, transportation, and customer service, the demand for specialists who can develop, implement, and optimize these technologies will soar. AI engineers, data scientists, and machine learning architects will be instrumental in driving innovation and efficiency.

The Rise of AI and Machine Learning Specialists: Pioneering Innovation in 2025

In the ever-evolving landscape of technology, Artificial Intelligence (AI) and Machine Learning have emerged as transformative forces across industries. As we look ahead to 2025, the demand for AI and Machine Learning Specialists is set to skyrocket, driving innovation, efficiency, and competitiveness in various sectors.

The Role of AI and Machine Learning Specialists

AI and Machine Learning Specialists are at the forefront of developing, implementing, and optimizing intelligent systems that can learn from data, make predictions, and automate tasks. Their expertise is instrumental in harnessing the power of data to derive actionable insights, enhance decision-making processes, and drive business outcomes.

Key Responsibilities

1. Algorithm Development: Specialists in AI and Machine Learning are adept at designing and refining algorithms that power intelligent systems. They develop algorithms for tasks such as pattern recognition, natural language processing, image recognition, and predictive analytics.

2. Data Analysis and Model Building: These professionals analyze large datasets, extract meaningful patterns, and build predictive models using machine learning techniques. They employ tools like Python, R, TensorFlow, and PyTorch to create models that can make accurate predictions and recommendations.

3. Deployment and Optimization: AI and Machine Learning Specialists are responsible for deploying models into production environments and optimizing their performance. They fine-tune algorithms, conduct A/B testing, and implement feedback loops to continuously improve model accuracy and efficiency.

4. Ethical and Responsible AI: With the growing importance of ethical AI practices, specialists in this field ensure that AI systems are developed and deployed responsibly, considering factors such as bias mitigation, fairness, transparency, and accountability.

Industry Impact

The impact of AI and Machine Learning extends across various industries:

Machine Learning Specialists are driving personalized marketing campaigns, recommendation engines, inventory optimization, and supply chain management in the retail and e-commerce space.

- **Manufacturing**: In manufacturing, AI is utilized for predictive maintenance, quality control, process optimization, and autonomous robotic systems.

Skills and Qualifications

To excel as an AI and Machine Learning Specialist, individuals require a strong foundation in mathematics, statistics, programming, and data analysis. Key skills include proficiency in programming languages like Python and R, knowledge of machine learning algorithms and techniques, experience with data preprocessing and feature engineering, and the ability to work with big data platforms and tools.

As we approach 2025, the demand for AI and Machine Learning Specialists will continue to grow, driven by the increasing reliance on data-driven decision-making, automation, and intelligent systems. These professionals are instrumental in unlocking the full potential of AI technology and shaping the future of innovation across industries.

2. **Cybersecurity Experts**: As digital threats become more sophisticated, the need for cybersecurity professionals will continue to grow. Cybersecurity analysts, ethical hackers, and information security managers will play pivotal roles in safeguarding sensitive data, networks, and systems against cyberattacks.

Safeguarding the Digital Frontier: The Vital Role of Cybersecurity Experts in 2025

In an era defined by digital connectivity and technological advancements, cybersecurity has become a paramount concern for individuals, businesses, and governments alike. As we look ahead to 2025, the demand for Cybersecurity Experts is poised to soar, driven by the evolving threat landscape and the critical need to protect sensitive data, networks, and systems.

The Crucial Role of Cybersecurity Experts

Cybersecurity Experts play a pivotal role in safeguarding organizations against a myriad of cyber threats, ranging from data breaches and ransomware attacks to phishing scams and insider threats. Their expertise encompasses a wide range of domains, including network security, application security, information security, and incident response.

Key Responsibilities

1. Security Architecture and Design:
   Cybersecurity Experts design robust security architectures that encompass firewalls, intrusion detection systems, encryption protocols, access control mechanisms, and secure network configurations. They ensure that systems are resilient against external threats and unauthorized access.

2. Vulnerability Assessment and Penetration Testing (VAPT):
These professionals conduct comprehensive assessments to identify vulnerabilities in systems, networks, and applications. They perform penetration testing to simulate cyberattacks and uncover potential weaknesses that could be exploited by malicious actors.

3. Security Operations and Incident Response: Cybersecurity Experts monitor networks and systems for suspicious activities, anomalies, and security breaches. They develop and implement incident response plans to swiftly mitigate threats, contain breaches, and restore normal operations in the event of a cyber incident.

4. Security Compliance and Governance: Ensuring compliance with industry regulations and standards is a key aspect of cybersecurity. Experts in this field navigate regulatory frameworks, implement security policies and procedures, conduct audits, and provide guidance on risk management and compliance best practices.

Industry Impact

The impact of Cybersecurity Experts spans across industries and sectors:

- Financial Services
In the financial sector, cybersecurity is paramount for protecting sensitive financial data, securing online transactions, and combating fraud and identity theft.

- Healthcare: In healthcare, Cybersecurity Experts safeguard electronic health records (EHRs), medical devices, and telehealth platforms, ensuring patient confidentiality and data integrity.

- Critical Infrastructure
Experts in cybersecurity play a critical role in protecting essential infrastructure such as power grids, transportation systems, and water treatment facilities from cyber threats that could disrupt operations and public services.

- Government and Defense:
Cybersecurity is a national security imperative, and experts in this field work to defend government networks, secure classified information, and counter cyber espionage and cyber warfare threats.

Skills and Qualifications

To excel as a Cybersecurity Expert, individuals need a strong foundation in information security principles, risk management, ethical hacking, and cybersecurity technologies. Key skills include proficiency in cybersecurity tools and platforms, knowledge of threat intelligence and analysis, experience with security incident response procedures, and the ability to stay updated on emerging threats and trends in the cybersecurity landscape.

As we advance into 2025, the role of Cybersecurity Experts will be indispensable in mitigating cyber risks, protecting digital assets, and ensuring the resilience of organizations in the face of evolving cyber threats. Their expertise and vigilance are essential in safeguarding the digital frontier and maintaining trust and security in an increasingly interconnected world.

3. Data Analysts and Data Scientists:

The era of big data is here to stay, making data analysts and scientists indispensable in extracting meaningful insights from vast datasets. These professionals will be instrumental in guiding strategic decisions, identifying trends, and enhancing operational efficiencies across industries.
The Impact of Data Analysts and Data Scientists in 2025
In the age of information, data has become the lifeblood of decision-making and innovation across industries. As we approach 2025, the demand for Data

Analysts and Data Scientists continues to escalate, driven by the exponential growth of data and the imperative to extract actionable insights from it.

The Significance of Data Analysts and Data Scientists
Data Analysts and Data Scientists are instrumental in transforming raw data into meaningful insights, predictive models, and data-driven strategies. Their expertise lies in analyzing complex datasets, identifying trends and patterns, and leveraging advanced analytics techniques to derive valuable business intelligence.

Key Responsibilities

1. Data Collection and Preparation:
Data Analysts and Data Scientists gather, clean, and preprocess data from various sources, ensuring its quality, integrity, and compatibility for analysis. They utilize tools like SQL, Python, R, and data visualization platforms to handle large datasets efficiently.

2. **Exploratory Data Analysis (EDA):**
These professionals conduct exploratory data analysis to uncover correlations, anomalies, and insights within the data. They use statistical methods, data mining techniques, and visualization tools to gain a deep understanding of the underlying patterns and relationships.

3. **Machine Learning and Predictive Modeling:** Data Scientists specialize in building predictive models and machine learning algorithms that can make accurate forecasts, classifications, and recommendations. They employ techniques such as regression analysis, clustering, decision trees, and neural networks to solve complex problems and drive predictive analytics initiatives.

4. **Business Intelligence and Decision Support:** Data Analysts and Data Scientists translate data insights into actionable recommendations and strategies for business stakeholders. They create dashboards, reports, and data visualizations that enable informed decision-making, performance tracking, and strategic planning.

Industry Impact

The impact of Data Analysts and Data Scientists spans across diverse industries and domains:

- **Retail and E-commerce:** In retail, these professionals optimize pricing strategies, analyze customer behavior, and personalize marketing campaigns based on data-driven insights and predictive analytics.

- **Healthcare**: In healthcare, Data Analysts and Data Scientists analyze patient data, optimize healthcare delivery, and contribute to clinical research, disease prevention, and personalized medicine initiatives.

- **Finance and Banking**: These experts in data analytics drive risk management, fraud detection, customer segmentation, and investment strategies in the finance sector, leveraging data-driven decision-making processes.

- **Manufacturing and Supply Chain**: Data analytics and predictive modeling are utilized in manufacturing for demand forecasting, inventory optimization, predictive maintenance, and supply chain efficiency improvements.

Skills and Qualifications

To excel as a Data Analyst or Data Scientist, individuals need a blend of technical skills, domain knowledge, and analytical acumen. Key skills include proficiency in programming languages like Python, R, SQL, and data manipulation tools, expertise in statistical analysis and machine learning algorithms, experience with data visualization and storytelling, and the ability to communicate complex findings effectively to non-technical stakeholders.

As we enter 2025, the role of Data Analysts and Data Scientists will continue to be pivotal in unlocking the value of data, driving innovation, and shaping data-driven strategies across industries. Their ability to harness the power of data and turn it into actionable insights will be instrumental in navigating the complexities of the digital age and driving business success in an increasingly data-centric world.

4.Healthcare Professionals:

The healthcare sector will see a surge in demand for various roles, including nurses, physicians, medical technicians, and healthcare administrators. Additionally, telemedicine specialists and experts in healthcare analytics will be in high demand as digital health solutions continue to evolve.

The Role of Renewable Energy Specialists in 2025

As the world transitions towards sustainable energy sources, Renewable Energy Specialists are poised to play a crucial role in shaping the future of energy production and consumption. With the global focus on reducing carbon emissions and mitigating climate change, the demand for Renewable Energy Specialists is expected to surge in 2025 and beyond.

The Importance of Renewable Energy Specialists

Renewable Energy Specialists are experts in harnessing renewable resources such as solar, wind, hydroelectric, geothermal, and biomass energy. Their expertise lies in designing, implementing, and optimizing renewable energy systems that reduce environmental impact, enhance energy efficiency, and promote sustainability.

Key Responsibilities

1. **Renewable Energy System Design:**
Specialists in renewable energy design systems that harness solar, wind, or other renewable sources to generate electricity or heat. They analyze factors such as resource availability, site suitability, technology feasibility, and energy storage solutions to design efficient and cost-effective systems.

2. **Project Development and Implementation:** Renewable Energy Specialists oversee the development and implementation of renewable energy projects, from feasibility studies and permitting to construction and commissioning. They collaborate with engineers, environmental experts, and stakeholders to ensure projects meet regulatory requirements and sustainability goals.

3. **Performance Monitoring and Optimization:**
These professionals monitor the performance of renewable energy systems, conduct data analysis, and implement optimization strategies to maximize energy output, reliability, and lifespan. They may utilize advanced monitoring tools, predictive analytics, and maintenance protocols to ensure optimal system performance.

4. **Research and Innovation:**
Renewable Energy Specialists contribute to research and innovation in renewable energy technologies, exploring new concepts, materials, and methodologies to improve efficiency, reduce costs, and overcome technical challenges in renewable energy deployment.

Industry Impact

The impact of Renewable Energy Specialists extends across various sectors and applications:

- **Power Generation**: In the energy sector, these professionals contribute to the expansion of renewable energy capacity through the development of solar farms, wind farms, hydroelectric projects, and other renewable energy installations.

- **Buildings and Infrastructure:**
Renewable Energy Specialists work on integrating renewable energy systems into buildings, communities, and infrastructure projects, such as solar panels on rooftops, geothermal heating and cooling systems, and energy-efficient designs.

- **Transportation**: Specialists in renewable energy also play a role in advancing electric vehicles (EVs) and sustainable transportation solutions powered by renewable energy sources, reducing reliance on fossil fuels in the transportation sector.

- **Environmental Sustainability**: By promoting the adoption of renewable energy technologies, Renewable Energy Specialists contribute to reducing greenhouse gas emissions, mitigating climate change impacts, and preserving natural resources for future generations.

Skills and Qualifications

To excel as a Renewable Energy Specialist, individuals need a combination of technical expertise, environmental knowledge, project management skills, and regulatory understanding. Key skills include proficiency in renewable energy technologies such as solar photovoltaics, wind turbines, and energy storage systems, familiarity with energy modeling and simulation software, understanding of energy policy and regulations, and a passion for environmental sustainability.

As we look ahead to 2025, the role of Renewable Energy Specialists will be instrumental in driving the transition towards a clean, sustainable energy future. Their contributions to renewable energy innovation, project development, and environmental stewardship will be pivotal in addressing global energy challenges and creating a more resilient and sustainable planet for generations to come.

5.Renewable Energy Specialists:

With a growing emphasis on sustainability and renewable energy sources, specialists in solar, wind, and other green technologies will be highly sought after. Jobs such as renewable energy engineers, sustainability consultants, and energy efficiency experts will be pivotal in driving the transition to a greener future.

Navigating the Virtual Workspace: The Rise of Remote Work Facilitators in 2025

The global shift towards remote and hybrid work models has reshaped the way we work, collaborate, and communicate. In 2025, Remote Work Facilitators will play a pivotal role in optimizing remote work environments, fostering collaboration, and ensuring productivity in distributed teams.

The Significance of Remote Work Facilitators

Remote Work Facilitators are professionals who specialize in creating and maintaining effective remote work ecosystems. They focus on enhancing communication, collaboration, workflow efficiency, and employee engagement in virtual work environments.

Key Responsibilities

1. **Virtual Collaboration Platforms:**

Remote Work Facilitators manage and optimize virtual collaboration platforms such as video conferencing tools, project management software, instant messaging platforms, and virtual whiteboards. They ensure that these tools are user-friendly, accessible, and conducive to efficient teamwork.

2. **Remote Team Management:**
These professionals provide guidance and support to remote teams, helping them navigate challenges, set clear goals, manage priorities, and foster a sense of camaraderie and belonging despite physical distance.

3. **Digital Workflow Optimization:**
Remote Work Facilitators streamline digital workflows, automate repetitive tasks, and implement efficient processes to enhance productivity and reduce bottlenecks in remote work settings. They may utilize workflow automation tools, task management systems, and agile methodologies to optimize team performance.

4. **Employee Engagement and Well-being**: Facilitators focus on promoting employee engagement, motivation, and well-being in remote teams. They organize virtual team-building activities, wellness initiatives, feedback sessions, and professional development opportunities to foster a positive remote work culture and mitigate burnout.

Industry Impact

The impact of Remote Work Facilitators spans across industries and sectors:

- **Technology**: In the tech industry, these professionals play a key role in enabling remote software development teams, agile project management, and collaboration among distributed engineering teams.

- **Finance and Banking**: Remote Work Facilitators contribute to virtual client meetings, remote financial services, digital banking solutions, and cybersecurity measures to protect sensitive data in remote work environments.

- **Healthcare**: In healthcare, facilitators support telemedicine initiatives, remote patient care coordination, and virtual healthcare consultations while ensuring compliance with regulatory requirements and patient privacy standards.

- **Education**: Facilitators in the education sector facilitate virtual classrooms, online learning platforms, remote student engagement, and digital teaching resources for distance education programs.

Skills and Qualifications

To excel as a Remote Work Facilitator, individuals need a combination of technical skills, communication skills, project management expertise, and a deep understanding of remote work dynamics. Key skills include proficiency in virtual collaboration tools, strong interpersonal and leadership skills, experience with remote team management, knowledge of cybersecurity best practices, and the ability to adapt to evolving technologies and work practices.

As remote and hybrid work models become the norm in 2025, the role of Remote Work Facilitators will be instrumental in driving productivity, fostering collaboration, and promoting employee well-being in virtual work environments. Their ability to leverage technology, build cohesive remote teams, and facilitate seamless communication will be essential in navigating the challenges and opportunities of the digital workspace.

6. E-commerce and Digital Marketing Professionals:

The rise of e-commerce platforms and digital marketing channels has created a demand for professionals skilled in e-commerce management, digital advertising, SEO/SEM, and social media marketing. Businesses are increasingly relying on digital strategies to reach and engage their target audiences.

Pioneering Innovation: The Role of Blockchain Developers and Cryptocurrency Experts in 2025

Blockchain technology and cryptocurrencies have revolutionized the digital landscape, offering decentralized solutions, secure transactions, and new avenues for innovation. In 2025, Blockchain Developers and Cryptocurrency Experts will be at the forefront of driving blockchain adoption, developing decentralized applications (dApps), and shaping the future of finance and technology.

The Significance of Blockchain Developers and Cryptocurrency Experts

Blockchain Developers specialize in designing, building, and maintaining blockchain-based systems, smart contracts, and decentralized applications. Cryptocurrency Experts, on the other hand, focus on understanding digital currencies, market trends, trading strategies, and the broader ecosystem of blockchain-based assets.

Key Responsibilities

1. **Blockchain Development**:
Developers in this field design and implement blockchain protocols, consensus mechanisms, and distributed ledger technologies (DLTs). They code smart contracts using languages like Solidity, develop blockchain architectures, and ensure the security and scalability of blockchain networks.

2. **Decentralized Applications (dApps)**:
Blockchain Developers create decentralized applications (dApps) that run on blockchain platforms such as Ethereum, Binance Smart Chain, and Polkadot. These dApps span various domains, including finance, supply chain, healthcare, gaming, and identity management.

3. **Cryptocurrency Development and Management:**
Cryptocurrency Experts are involved in the creation, management, and governance of digital currencies and tokens. They understand blockchain economics, tokenomics, consensus algorithms, and cryptocurrency protocols

4. **Blockchain Integration and Adoption**:
These professionals work on integrating blockchain technology into existing systems, platforms, and industries. They collaborate with businesses, governments, and organizations to explore use cases, pilot projects, and initiatives that leverage blockchain for transparency, security, and efficiency.

Industry Impact

The impact of Blockchain Developers and Cryptocurrency Experts extends across diverse sectors and applications:

- **Finance and Banking**: In the financial sector, these professionals drive innovation in payments, remittances, decentralized finance (DeFi), asset tokenization, and digital identity verification using blockchain technology.

- **Supply Chain and Logistics**: Blockchain is utilized for supply chain traceability, provenance tracking, transparent transactions, and combating counterfeit products, with experts in this field enabling blockchain adoption in logistics and supply chain management.

- **Healthcare**: In healthcare, blockchain technology facilitates secure medical records management, interoperability between healthcare systems, pharmaceutical supply chain transparency, and patient data privacy, with experts ensuring compliance and data integrity.

- **Gaming and NFTs**: Blockchain Developers and Cryptocurrency Experts contribute to the development of blockchain-based games, non-fungible tokens (NFTs), digital collectibles, and virtual economies, transforming the gaming and entertainment industries.

Skills and Qualifications

To excel as a Blockchain Developer or Cryptocurrency Expert, individuals need a strong foundation in computer science, cryptography, blockchain technologies, and digital finance. Key skills include proficiency in blockchain development platforms (e.g., Ethereum, Hyperledger), smart contract programming, knowledge of cryptocurrency exchanges and wallets, understanding of consensus algorithms, and familiarity with regulatory frameworks.

As we enter 2025, the role of Blockchain Developers and Cryptocurrency Experts will be instrumental in driving blockchain innovation, fostering decentralized ecosystems, and unlocking new possibilities in digital finance, governance, and technology. Their expertise in blockchain development, cryptocurrency management, and industry adoption will shape the future of decentralized applications, digital assets, and the broader blockchain ecosystem.

7. Remote Work Facilitators:

The shift towards remote and hybrid work models has highlighted the need for professionals who can facilitate seamless remote collaboration. Roles such as remote team managers, virtual collaboration specialists, and digital workspace architects will be essential in ensuring productivity and connectivity in distributed work environments.

Innovating the Future: The Impact of Robotics Engineers and Automation Specialists in 2025

The era of automation and robotics has ushered in a new wave of technological advancement, transforming industries, enhancing productivity, and reshaping the way we work. In 2025, Robotics Engineers and Automation Specialists will be instrumental in driving innovation, deploying robotic systems, and optimizing automated processes across diverse sectors.

The Importance of Robotics Engineers and Automation Specialists

Robotics Engineers specialize in designing, developing, and deploying robotic systems that perform tasks autonomously or semi-autonomously. Automation Specialists, on the other hand, focus on optimizing and streamlining processes through the use of automated solutions, software, and technologies.

Key Responsibilities

1. **Robotics System Design**: Robotics Engineers design robotic systems, including robotic arms, drones, autonomous vehicles, industrial robots, and robotic prototypes. They consider factors such as mechanical design, sensors, actuators, control systems, and human-robot interaction to create efficient and safe robotic solutions.

2. **Programming and Control**: These professionals program and configure robotic systems using languages such as C++, Python, ROS (Robot Operating System), and PLC (Programmable Logic Controller) languages. They develop

algorithms for motion planning, object recognition, path optimization, and robot behavior.

3. **Integration and Deployment**: Robotics Engineers and Automation Specialists integrate robotic systems into existing workflows, production lines, and operational environments. They collaborate with stakeholders, conduct testing and validation, and ensure seamless deployment and operation of robotic solutions.

4. **Process Automation and Optimization**: Automation Specialists focus on automating repetitive tasks, workflows, and processes using software automation tools, robotic process automation (RPA), artificial intelligence (AI), and machine learning (ML). They analyze workflows, identify automation opportunities, and implement solutions to improve efficiency and reduce human error.

Industry Impact

The impact of Robotics Engineers and Automation Specialists spans across various industries and applications:

- **Manufacturing**: In manufacturing, these professionals automate production processes, assembly lines, quality control inspections, and material handling tasks using industrial robots and automation technologies, improving productivity and reducing costs.

- **Logistics and Warehousing**: Robotics and automation play a key role in logistics and warehousing operations, with specialists optimizing inventory management, order fulfillment, picking and packing processes, and autonomous logistics solutions.

- **Healthcare**: Robotics Engineers contribute to medical robotics, surgical robots, assistive technologies, and automation in healthcare delivery, while Automation Specialists focus on streamlining administrative tasks, patient data management, and telemedicine workflows.

- **Agriculture**: In agriculture, robotics and automation specialists work on autonomous farming equipment, precision agriculture solutions, crop monitoring drones, and robotic harvesters to increase agricultural efficiency and sustainability.

Skills and Qualifications

To excel as a Robotics Engineer or Automation Specialist, individuals need a blend of technical skills, domain knowledge, problem-solving abilities, and a strong understanding of robotics, automation technologies, and industrial processes. Key skills include proficiency in robotics programming languages, familiarity with automation tools and platforms, knowledge of sensors and actuators, experience with robotic simulations and testing, and a collaborative mindset for cross-functional teamwork.

As we move forward into 2025, Robotics Engineers and Automation Specialists will continue to drive innovation, efficiency, and competitiveness across industries. Their expertise in robotics, automation, and process optimization will be essential in navigating the complexities of the digital age and leveraging technology to create a more productive and sustainable future.

8. Blockchain Developers and Cryptocurrency Experts:

As blockchain technology continues to disrupt various industries, the demand for blockchain developers, smart contract engineers, and cryptocurrency analysts is expected to rise. These professionals will drive innovation in fintech, supply chain management, healthcare, and beyond.

Shaping a Sustainable Future: The Role of Environmental Scientists and Climate Change Analysts in 2025

As the world faces pressing environmental challenges and strives towards sustainability, Environmental Scientists and Climate Change Analysts will play a pivotal role in understanding, mitigating, and adapting to the impacts of climate change. In 2025, their expertise will be in high demand as societies and industries seek solutions for a greener and more resilient future.

The Importance of Environmental Scientists and Climate Change Analysts

Environmental Scientists focus on studying the natural environment, ecosystems, and human impact on the planet. Climate Change Analysts specialize in assessing climate data, modeling climate scenarios, and evaluating the risks and opportunities associated with climate change mitigation and adaptation strategies.

Key Responsibilities

1. **Environmental Research and Analysis**: Environmental Scientists conduct research, collect data, and analyze environmental factors such as air quality, water resources, biodiversity, land use, and pollution. They use scientific methods, models, and GIS (Geographic Information Systems) to assess environmental conditions and trends.

2. **Climate Modeling and Analysis**: Climate Change Analysts model climate patterns, analyze climate data, and assess the impacts of climate change on ecosystems, communities, infrastructure, and economies. They evaluate scenarios, risks, vulnerabilities, and potential adaptation measures to address climate challenges.

3. **Sustainability Assessment**: These professionals assess sustainability practices, evaluate environmental policies and regulations, and recommend strategies for sustainable resource management, conservation, and renewable energy adoption. They work towards achieving environmental sustainability goals and reducing ecological footprints.

4. **Climate Change Mitigation and Adaptation**: Environmental Scientists and Climate Change Analysts collaborate on developing and implementing climate change mitigation strategies, such as carbon reduction initiatives, renewable

energy projects, green infrastructure development, and sustainable transportation solutions. They also focus on adaptation measures to cope with climate impacts such as sea-level rise, extreme weather events, and ecosystem shifts.

Industry Impact

The impact of Environmental Scientists and Climate Change Analysts spans across various sectors and domains:

- **Energy and Utilities:** These professionals contribute to renewable energy development, carbon emissions reduction strategies, energy efficiency programs, and climate-resilient infrastructure in the energy and utilities sector.

- **Urban Planning and Development**: In urban areas, they work on sustainable city planning, green building design, urban forestry initiatives, water management projects, and climate-responsive urban development.

- **Natural Resource Management**: Environmental Scientists and Analysts play a role in natural resource conservation, wildlife protection, sustainable agriculture practices, and ecosystem restoration projects in forestry, fisheries, and wildlife management.

- **Corporate Sustainability**: Many businesses and corporations hire these experts to develop corporate sustainability strategies, conduct environmental impact assessments, comply with environmental regulations, and engage in responsible business practices.

Skills and Qualifications

To excel as an Environmental Scientist or Climate Change Analyst, individuals need a strong foundation in environmental science, climate science, data analysis, and sustainability principles. Key skills include proficiency in statistical analysis and modeling, knowledge of environmental laws and regulations, experience with GIS and remote sensing technologies, effective communication skills for stakeholder engagement, and a passion for environmental stewardship.

As we approach 2025, the expertise of Environmental Scientists and Climate Change Analysts will be indispensable in addressing global environmental challenges, fostering sustainability, and building resilience to climate change impacts. Their work contributes to creating a more sustainable and livable planet for current and future generations, highlighting the critical importance of their roles in shaping a greener and more resilient future.

09: Environmental Scientists and Climate Change Analysts:

With growing concerns about climate change and environmental sustainability, the demand for environmental scientists, climate change analysts, and sustainability researchers will increase. These professionals will work towards developing solutions to mitigate environmental impact and promote sustainable practices.

Safeguarding Data and Securing Systems: The Vital Role of Data Privacy and Cybersecurity Experts in 2025

In an era dominated by digital interactions and data-driven technologies, the protection of sensitive information and the security of digital systems have become paramount concerns. As we advance into 2025, the demand for Data

Privacy and Cybersecurity Experts is expected to surge, driven by the evolving threat landscape and the increasing importance of data protection regulations.

The Significance of Data Privacy and Cybersecurity Experts

Data Privacy and Cybersecurity Experts are professionals who specialize in safeguarding data, securing digital systems, and ensuring compliance with privacy regulations. They play a crucial role in mitigating cyber threats, protecting sensitive information, and maintaining trust in digital interactions.

Key Responsibilities

1. **Data Privacy Compliance**: Experts in this field ensure that organizations comply with data privacy regulations such as GDPR (General Data Protection Regulation), CCPA (California Consumer Privacy Act), and other regional or industry-specific privacy laws. They develop and implement privacy policies, conduct privacy impact assessments, and monitor data handling practices to protect consumer privacy rights.

2. **Cyber Threat Detection and Prevention**: Cybersecurity Experts focus on detecting, preventing, and responding to cyber threats such as malware, ransomware, phishing attacks, and data breaches. They employ security measures such as firewalls, intrusion detection systems, endpoint protection, and security incident response protocols to safeguard digital assets and sensitive data.

3. **Security Awareness Training**: These professionals conduct security awareness training programs for employees, educating them about cybersecurity best practices, phishing awareness, social engineering threats, and data protection protocols. They promote a culture of cybersecurity awareness and vigilance within organizations.

4. **Incident Response and Forensics**: Data Privacy and Cybersecurity Experts are involved in incident response planning, cybersecurity incident investigations, digital forensics analysis, and remediation efforts following security breaches or data incidents. They collaborate with legal teams, IT

departments, and law enforcement agencies to manage cyber incidents effectively.

Industry Impact

The impact of Data Privacy and Cybersecurity Experts spans across various industries and sectors:

- **Finance and Banking**: In the financial sector, these professionals safeguard financial transactions, protect customer data, combat fraud, and ensure compliance with financial regulations such as PCI DSS (Payment Card Industry Data Security Standard).

- **Healthcare**: In healthcare, Data Privacy and Cybersecurity Experts protect electronic health records (EHRs), medical devices, and patient information, ensuring HIPAA (Health Insurance Portability and Accountability Act) compliance and data confidentiality.

- **Technology and IT Services**: These experts secure digital platforms, cloud infrastructure, software applications, and IT systems, mitigating cyber risks and ensuring data integrity, availability, and confidentiality.

- **Government and Defense**: In government and defense sectors, cybersecurity experts protect national security assets, critical infrastructure, classified information, and sensitive government data from cyber threats and espionage.

Skills and Qualifications

To excel as a Data Privacy or Cybersecurity Expert, individuals need a strong technical foundation in information security, risk management, compliance, and privacy regulations. Key skills include proficiency in security technologies and tools, knowledge of threat intelligence analysis, incident response planning, penetration testing, ethical hacking, and communication skills for effective collaboration and stakeholder engagement.

As we navigate the digital age and the complexities of cybersecurity threats, the expertise of Data Privacy and Cybersecurity Experts will be indispensable in safeguarding data, protecting digital assets, and maintaining trust in digital interactions. Their role in mitigating cyber risks, ensuring compliance with privacy regulations, and promoting cybersecurity awareness will be instrumental in building resilient and secure digital ecosystems in 2025 and beyond.

Summary

In conclusion, the job market of 2025 will be characterized by a demand for specialized skills that align with technological advancements, industry trends, and societal priorities. Professionals who possess expertise in areas such as cybersecurity, data analysis, renewable energy, remote work facilitation, blockchain technology, environmental science, and data privacy will be highly sought after.

Adaptability, continuous learning, and a willingness to embrace new technologies will be key for professionals seeking to thrive in this dynamic landscape. The rapid pace of technological innovation, coupled with evolving industry needs and global challenges, requires individuals to stay updated with the latest trends, acquire new skills, and adapt to changing work environments.

Moreover, interdisciplinary skills and the ability to collaborate across diverse teams and industries will be valuable assets. As industries converge and new opportunities emerge at the intersection of technology, sustainability, and social impact, professionals who can navigate complex challenges, foster innovation, and drive positive change will be in high demand.

The job market of 2025 presents exciting opportunities for individuals who are proactive, versatile, and committed to lifelong learning. By staying agile, embracing innovation, and honing specialized skills, professionals can position themselves for success in a rapidly evolving and competitive global economy.

www.ingramcontent.com/pod-product-compliance
Lightning Source LLC
Chambersburg PA
CBHW070958220526
45471CB00007B/3083